JEN LOCKET

by Christine Simpson

Pearl Press

Special thanks to these people
for going above and beyond the call

Laura Almada

Ann Marie Brown

John Czajkowski

Marian Durkee

Betty Miller

Carol Ritter

JENNY'S LOCKET
Copyright © 1996 by Christine Simpson
Illustrations by Preston Hindmarch
Aardvark Graphics, Easton, PA
Typeset by Almada Illustrations, Grosse Ile, MI

Published by Pearl Press
Nazareth, PA 18064
800-335-6881

Printed and bound in the United States
ISBN 0-9643245-0-4
Library of Congress Catalog Card Number: 94-90538

Jenny's Locket is my family's true story about Paul. While the use of diary entries is a literary, stylistic tool, the content thereof accurately reflects the occurrences of Jenny's life. No excerpts are taken from my daughter's personal diary, the privacy of which I respect. -- CPS

In loving memory of
Paul Rupp Simpson
November 4, 1953 - February 14, 1992

He lived with love,
Fought with courage,
And died with dignity.

We miss you.

This book is dedicated to my husband, Robin,
whose devotion and selflessness
to his brother, Paul, was unsurpassed

and to my children, Jenny and Teddy,
whose bravery overcame their fear
to allow our story to be shared.

My name is Jenny. I am eleven years old and I am finally in sixth grade. It feels terrific to be the "King of the Hill!" After all these years, it is my class's turn to rule the roost. I absolutely love school and, as long as I can remember, I always have. So far this year I have all A's on my report card. My parents tell me not to put so much pressure on myself, but I want to do well! Sounds pretty crazy, doesn't it? Yet it is the truth. I truly love school. After school I volunteer as a tutor twice a week, helping younger students with their school work. I like to help others, but I don't think I'll be a teacher when I'm older. I'm not sure what I want to do. In the meantime, I'm also busy with Scouts, drama, and chorus. My life is pretty active — just the way I like it!

My favorite thing in the whole wide world is to cheer for my local peewee football team. Oh, I was so happy when I made the squad four years ago. This year I made captain! As you can imagine, I am in seventh heaven. During the fall we have football games every weekend. If you want to find me on a Sunday afternoon, just go to the peewees' football field and look for the black and red uniforms! That's where I'll be — yelling at the top of my voice. I feel terrific in my cheerleading uniform. Fall is definitely a favorite time of year for me.

Apart from cheerleading, I love to ski, read, write in my diary, and talk on the telephone. Sometimes my parents think I was born with a telephone attached to my ear! I get angry with my parents because they won't let me on the telephone after 9:00 at night. I think it is a dumb rule. However, no matter how much I complain about it, they won't change their minds. That sure is frustrating. If I can't talk after 9:00 at night, I'd settle for a phone in my bedroom. That would be a dream come true! You guessed it — they won't allow that either. So, for now, I borrow the portable phone and hide with it in my bedroom. My parents do not mind as long as I return it. At least I have privacy. Boy, do I love to talk on the phone! There just don't seem to be enough hours in the day to call everyone I want to talk to. My friends are very special to me.

My favorite piece of jewelry is a beautiful, golden heart-shaped locket that hangs on a long golden chain. It is very precious to me. Although I don't wear it every day, it helps me feel happy. It comforts me to know I have this locket and that I can wear it whenever I want. I know I will have it for the rest of my life.

2

> *Dear Diary,*
>
> *I am so excited. Mom and Dad finally let me perm my hair. It is about time! I have bugged them for months about getting one. I LOVE the curls. Do I ever look different! It is weird seeing myself in the mirror. Even my parents like my hair. Mom says I look about 15 years old. I can't wait to go to school tomorrow and show all my friends. Now, if only my eyes were blue.... I don't like my hazel eyes. I think blue eyes go much better with blond hair. Isn't it a bummer that you can't choose your looks?*
>
> *Good night.*
> *Jenny*

I have a younger brother named Teddy. He has blue eyes and blond hair! I don't think it is fair that Ted has my blue eyes. He doesn't even think about the color of his eyes. They could be fluorescent purple for all he cares!

Sometimes I love Teddy and sometimes I hate him. It has nothing to do with the fact that he has the blue eyes I want. It has everything to do with having a younger brother! Teddy is eight and is in third grade. We go to the same school, but we won't next year. Freedom is on its way! In the morning our friends stop by our house to pick up Teddy and me on their way to school. We live only two blocks from our school, so we walk every day. It is nice to have a big crowd accompany us to school.

Teddy does not like school as much as I do, but still he does all right. He is pretty smart and gets decent grades. What he absolutely loves is Nintendo! Every day after school he rushes home to pop in a game! Mom is pretty strict about Nintendo and TV. Besides, if she is not working, Mom really likes to talk with us when we get home. On those days, Ted's Nintendo waits until much later in the evening. It is pretty obvious that my brother would spend his entire day in front of a Nintendo if my parents would let him. Teddy doesn't like to read as much as I do. When he does read, it is usually a Nintendo magazine! As I said, my brother really likes electronics!

My parents make a real effort to get Teddy away from television. This year, my brother plays football, wrestles, plays T-ball, and skis. Because Ted is big and strong for his age, his football coach put him on the defensive line. He plays left guard — number 74! When Ted suits up in his white uniform and pads, he looks huge. I am proud of him and I often tell him. That makes him happy. Teddy is on a younger team, so I do not cheer for him. That would be awesome, though!

Ted Simpson, he's our man!

If he can't do it, no one can!

Mom and Dad come to the football field on Sunday afternoons to watch both Ted and me. They are there every week — for hours! It is great fun. After the games, Ted and I attack the food stand. My brother usually goes home with a gallon of ketchup on his white jersey from all his hot dogs and french fries! Often he is messier from eating than from playing football!

After football season, we head into other sports and activities. Teddy loves winter as much as I do. We find lots to do in the snow. Snow forts and snowballs are high on our list. So is skiing.

Dear Diary,

A wonderful day! Tonight I went ski-ing. Teddy finally learned how to ski the black diamonds! Those are the expert slopes. Yahoo!

Dad couldn't come, but Mom did. So did my best friend, Mya. I'm sorry Dad wasn't with us — he is a blast on the slopes. He doesn't mind going fast, but I can still go faster! Not to brag, but I am the best skier in our family. Mom is a bit of a scaredy-cat!

Tonight Teddy, Mya, and I lost her on purpose. We headed for the expert slope and she wouldn't follow us! Mom just laughed at us as we disappeared down the black diamond. She told me later that there was no way she was going down that cliff! Well, I'm sleepy and tired right now.

Talk to you later.
Jenny

I love my parents. Dad is a judge and Mom is a school psychologist. We spend much time together as a family. I know my parents care about my brother and me. We live in a brick house in a small town in Pennsylvania. I have a pink and green bedroom with its own bathroom. When I think about all that I have, I feel pretty lucky. You may think my life sounds perfect, but it isn't. My Uncle Paul is dying of AIDS.

Uncle Paul is my father's younger brother. I absolutely adore him. He is thirty-eight years old and has blue eyes. Although he is my uncle, I usually call him Paul. He calls me "Jen-Jen." I like it when Paul calls me "Jen-Jen" because that is my special name just with him. When he writes to me,

Paul draws a heart around each "Jen" in a different color magic maker. It is cute.

Ever since I can remember, Paul has been special in our lives. He and Dad are the only kids in their family and they have always been close. I absolutely LOVE to hear Paul's stories about when Dad and he were younger. Believe me, Paul sure can tell whoppers! He has a great way of exaggerating the stories to make them especially interesting. Some of the best ones are about Mom. Paul and Mom met years ago when they were in high school. They have been friends ever since — very special friends. Sometimes I think Mom considers Paul her "real" brother because she does not have any brothers of her own. She has only sisters. Mom really loves my uncle.

The great part is that Paul went to the same school as my parents when they were dating! Mom and Dad are high school sweethearts. Paul was the typical, younger brother — always pestering and spying on his big brother! Boy, Teddy better not do that to me when I am older! My uncle never hesitates to tell Teddy and me the most embarrassing, exaggerated tales about Mom and Dad. They are wonderful! When Paul begins his stories, my parents just roll their eyes and groan. It sure is weird hearing about when my parents dated or what Dad was like as a little kid. Whenever I see Paul, I always beg him to tell me stories — even the ones I have heard a million times.

Dear Diary,

Not much happened today. Tonight I am just sitting in my room thinking about Paul. I wonder what it will be like not to hear Paul tell his stories anymore...and not to hear the name "Jen-Jen" anymore. Paul's always been a part of my life. Guess I always assumed he'd be there forever. But now he is really sick and weak. Paul is in the hospital almost continuously. Paul is dying. It isn't fair.

Things are lousy at home these days. I am very sad. So are Mom and Dad and Ted. Paul's fight with AIDS takes up our lives. Last week my parents did not make my football game. They won't this week either. They just landed that one on me at dinner. I hate what's happening. Mom and Dad are usually in New York every weekend with Paul, helping him battle his AIDS.

Even when Mom and Dad are home, they aren't available. Today they spent HOURS on the phone with Paul and his doctors and the hospital. That happens a

> *lot. I really miss my parents. I miss how it used to be. I hate that I'm losing Paul. I often cry myself to sleep. Tonight is one of those nights....*
>
> *I talk lots to Mom and Dad about Paul; but I am glad I have you, too, Diary.*
>
> > *Talk to you later.*
> > *Jen-Jen*

Years ago Paul told my parents the awful news about having AIDS. Mom and Dad didn't tell Teddy and me right away. I was only six and was just finishing kindergarten. Ted wasn't even in school yet. At that time, it was only a few years into the AIDS problem. People were really scared and treated AIDS patients and their relatives like outcasts. Many people still do. That frightens me. Because I was so young at the time, my parents waited until I was older before they told me the entire story. Teddy still doesn't know everything, but he will someday.

My parents did tell Teddy and me five years ago that Paul was dying. Mom and Dad explained that Paul had a deadly illness that would kill him someday. They warned us that we could get this disease from his blood. In order to protect ourselves, we were NEVER to touch Paul's blood. I took Mom and Dad's cautions seriously, but not their comments about his dying. Actually, I didn't believe them. How could Paul be dying when he looked and acted fine? Besides, he was too young. He was only thirty-two. So for a long time, I never thought much about my uncle's illness when we were together or apart.

Boy, has that changed. Paul doesn't look or act fine anymore, and I often think about his disease. Now he is very thin, is in constant pain, and has other illnesses he can't shake. Paul tries very hard to be happy when I talk to him on the phone, even though he is very weak and knows he is close to dying. I think my uncle is extremely brave.

Dear Diary,

Sometimes I shouldn't write a diary. I just read parts of my diary from last year. I found something I didn't want to find — the day my parents told me Paul had AIDS. It was an absolutely dreadful day.

I still remember those awful words that came out of their mouths. I still feel my heart jump into my throat. I still remember staring at my parents with my mouth wide open, not saying a word. I was so stunned.

10

> *Sure, I know about AIDS. I knew about it in fifth grade. We learn about it in school. But I never, never thought I had to worry about it in my family. Not in my nice professional family, in my nice brick house, in my nice small town in Pennsylvania. AIDS is some terrible disease killing lots of other people out in the world. Not people in my family. Not people I love. Not Paul.*
>
> *I never dreamed AIDS would affect my family. Boy, was I wrong. Even after a year, I still can't believe this is happening. Paul...AIDS...dying? It can't be true, but it is.*
>
> *Jen-Jen*

When my parents finally explained that Paul had AIDS, they told me what I already knew. AIDS stands for acquired immunodeficiency syndrome. It develops gradually in people diagnosed as HIV positive. HIV stands for human immunodeficiency virus. This virus leads to AIDS. Both HIV and AIDS are linked to the immune system.

All of us need an immune system to make us well when we get sick. If you are healthy, you have a good immune system. It fights diseases, infections, and germs — big and small — that invade your body. Several different parts of your immune system must work together to fight diseases effectively. This cooperative effort is directed by your "T cells."

T cells control your immune system. They are like "generals" in charge of everything. T cells give "instructions" to your immune system — just like generals give commands to an army. They tell your body to fight and how to fight an invasion of germs. Without T cells, your body does not kick into action against germs.

Unfortunately, HIV attacks and kills your T cells. As your T cells are gradually destroyed, your body fights disease less and less effectively because the "generals" are disappearing. Now your immune system receives fewer and fewer commands to fight diseases. The T cells remaining cannot keep up with the spread of germs. Your body cannot totally get rid of infections. As this occurs, you become sicker and weaker. Because you have many T cells, it takes a while for HIV to destroy them all. Therefore, it can take a long time to die — years. However, slowly and eventually the virus kills all your T cells. At last, they are all destroyed, leaving none in your body. Now there are no "generals" and no instructions telling your immune system what to do. Once your T cells are gone, nothing kicks your immune system into action when you get sick. Your body no longer makes even a weak attempt to fight infections. Diseases take over your body and, in time, you die.

Most AIDS patients die from a special type of pneumonia (PCP) or cancer (KS). However, there are twenty-five "opportunistic" infections. When you get one of these diseases, you are considered an AIDS patient. You are no longer regarded as "merely" HIV positive.

Dear Diary,

Just sitting here doodling. Trying not to think about Paul. That's a joke and a half. He's all I have thought about for days...and especially today. I've been wondering if he has HIV or if he has AIDS. My parents weren't that specific with me last year. I finally got up the courage ask Mom. Guess I shouldn't have. The answer is the pits.

Mom told me that years ago, when I was in kindergarten, Paul found out he was HIV positive. Now he has no T cells left. It took six years to destroy them all. When Mom first said that, six years seemed like a long time for something to disappear. But when I think about it,

13

> *what difference does that make now?*
> *His T cells are gone. Gone. No more.*
>
> *Mom also told me Paul has the special*
> *type of cancer and many other medical*
> *problems. The end is getting near. It is*
> *sad and scary to know that Paul is "offi-*
> *cially" an AIDS patient. I just never*
> *thought it would happen in my family.*
>
> *Guess I'm not really surprised to find*
> *out that Paul has AIDS. He hasn't looked*
> *or acted healthy for a while. He is so sick.*
> *Nothing can help him. Nothing. Not even*
> *my love for him.*
>
> *Love,*
> *Jenny*

There is no cure for HIV — or AIDS — at this time. Some medicines do slow down the HIV destruction of T cells. During the six years since Paul first discovered he had HIV, some medicines did help him. But even with the help of medication, Paul could not shake off HIV. Now he has moved into the AIDS stage. Without a cure, Paul will die *eventually.*

That was always the big word...*eventually.* It seemed that day would never come — especially for Paul who fights so hard and whom I love so much.

However, *eventually* is now here. As we all struggle with the final, difficult days of Paul's battle with AIDS, I find myself thinking about everything that has happened. I find myself remembering special memories of my favorite uncle.

Paul lives in New York City. I always loved it when he lived at 1 Fifth Avenue, before he moved uptown to 84th Street. To me, his first address always sounded so classy and romantic. So does calling his city "The Big Apple."

Ted and I are my uncle's only nephew and niece. I guess you could say he spoiled us. Often Paul would mail us the junkiest and cheapest toys from the streets of New York. Whenever Paul was out and about in the City, he kept his eye open for the latest cool toys — whether he was uptown, downtown, in the subways, or just on the streets. Big Apple toys are simply wonderful. You sure can't find them in Pennsylvania! Ted's favorite is the huge, hairy, jumping spider Paul bought for one dollar from a man in a subway. Oh, it is gross all right and Mom really hates it! We can always count on her to jump a mile high when we sneak it up on her. That's not easy to do. Out of self-defense, Mom grew "eyes" in the back of her head! That spider makes her crazy!

It was heaven to visit Paul in The Big Apple — at least before he was really sick. I still remember the first time Ted went to New York City. He was about four years old. As we drove to New York, Mom asked Ted if he thought there would be cows in New York. "Yes, Mommy," he replied. "There will be *lots* and *lots* of cows." I chuckled to myself because I knew better — I had already been to the City.

Boy, did Ted's eyes bug out going through the Lincoln Tunnel to get to Manhattan! He couldn't believe we were under a river. When we popped out the other side of the tunnel, Ted's mouth hung wide open looking at all the skyscrapers. He never had seen anything so tall. Teddy never missed the cows!

We planned fun trips with Paul when we were in New York. Once he met us at a museum and surprised us with a huge tin of popcorn. We attacked it right away and got in trouble with the museum guard! Often Paul took us on the subway to our favorite restaurant for foot-long hot dogs. The subway was a grand adventure; the hot dogs even better!

Dear Diary,

Just got off the phone with Paul. He is having a good day. Some days are definitely better than others. Tonight it was fun to talk. We laughed and laughed about when he used to visit us. They were the best *times.*

Paul was in hysterics laughing about all the times he misbehaved at our house. And there were plenty! He really was a ringleader! It never took him long to convince Teddy and me to misbehave with him. I can still hear Mom and Dad scolding Paul — just like a kid! But he would laugh at them and then do whatever he wanted. Guess it was like having three kids in the house whenever Paul was in town — only worse. Ted and I never would have done the things we did if Paul hadn't been there. NO WAY!

We sneaked cake for breakfast. Paul rented our favorite movies and "demanded" that Ted and I stay up really late with him. The chicken fights were fabulous. His answers for Mad Libs were totally outrageous. And Paul taught us not to eat "yellow snow" — and why! Mom and Dad always said it took Ted and me a week to calm down after Paul left! They were right, but it was worth it. Now I know why Mom and Dad never really stopped him.

Oh boy, we sure had fun. Such happy memories. It was great talking about

I especially remember last year when Paul visited us right before Halloween. We had a blast. Paul watched me march with my cheerleading squad in the Halloween parade. He whistled and shouted when I walked by him. I was so embarrassed — my entire football team was right behind me! Afterwards, Paul went back to our house and took a *long* nap. I did not understand why. He said the parade exhausted him. How tired can you get just sitting on a curb, watching a parade? I surely did not appreciate much about Paul's illness in fifth grade. I did not realize that the continual HIV attack on his body made daily life a constant effort. When I look back now, I marvel at Paul's brave fight against his disease. He seldom complained and never gave up the battle.

After Paul's snooze, the Halloween fun really began. That night we had a pumpkin carving contest. Dad bought five enormous pumpkins and we each carved our own. Mine wasn't too bad, but Paul's was *terrible!* It was lopsided and had a big howling mouth. Oh, how we howled when we saw

18

it! Paul tried to defend his pumpkin, saying he hadn't carved one in years. I'm sure that was true, but Paul's excuse did not fly with us. We were merciless — just as he would have been if the tables had been turned.

As always, Dad's pumpkin was extremely scary — complete with evil eyebrows and facial scars. Paul made some rather choice remarks about it. I was certain Dad's creation would win the judging contest, but it didn't. Teddy's happy, grinning, toothy pumpkin did. What shocked everyone was that *my* pumpkin lost the contest! Personally, I think Paul's whining won him a couple of sympathy votes. Huh! So much for fairness. As expected, Paul lorded his victory over me!

That night we started a new tradition. We placed a pumpkin in each of the five windows in the front of our house. From the outside our home, lit only by flickering pumpkins, looked dark and eerie. I put Paul's pumpkin in my bedroom window. It didn't matter to me that it was howling and lopsided. It was Paul's, and I liked whatever Paul did. I didn't sleep in my bedroom that night. My uncle did. Whenever Paul visited, he always stayed in my bedroom because I have a bathroom attached to it.

At first I used to get very nervous when Paul stayed in my room. Why was it always *my* bedroom? Then my parents told me more about Paul's disease. I felt much better. In fact, I was very relieved.

Dad took a long time explaining how I could get HIV or AIDS. He answered all my questions and made sure I understood. I truly realize that I can't get HIV or AIDS from Paul just because he sleeps on my mattress or uses my bathroom. I can't get it just from "being around him." Now that I think about it, we all use the same glasses, the same dishes, the same utensils whenever Paul is in town. Mom always kisses my uncle on the lips when she sees him. That definitely means Paul is safe because I know she would not take any chances.

Getting AIDS is not like catching a cold or the flu. There are very specific ways you get AIDS. You can get AIDS from contaminated blood or needles, unprotected sex with an infected person, or birthing or nursing involving an infected mother. We do keep plastic gloves in the house just in case Paul bleeds. We never have had to wear them, but they would protect us if we ever had to touch Paul's blood. And Dad always disinfects my bathroom after Paul leaves. It took me a while to figure out what all this information really meant. But now I certainly feel safe around my uncle.

Dear Diary,

Today we went over AIDS in school. Even so, a ton of rumors float around school about the disease. They make me mad. I wish people would learn the truth about HIV and AIDS. If they did, then they wouldn't spread rumors. And they wouldn't be afraid. And I wouldn't get scared by the things I hear in school. The rumors frighten me even though I know they aren't true. Why do people spread tales?

I am glad I can talk to my parents. I am glad they have answers. I hope other kids ask their parents, too. I hope other kids listen to the answers. I hope their parents have the right information. This is all so confusing...but it doesn't have to be....

Ta for now.
Jen

One of my last happy memories of my uncle occurred last summer about six months ago. Ted and I went to different scout camps for a week right before school started. It was my fourth year at camp; Ted's, first. Camp was extra great fun this year because three of my best friends went with me. The gang shared a tent together. It was awesome. After a week together, the four of us were still talking to each other! Our moms weren't so sure that would happen!

While Teddy and I were away, Paul unexpectedly visited my parents. I was sorry I wasn't home because I missed being with him. But the good news was that I received more mail than usual. When I am at camp, Mom writes me a letter every day. During Paul's visit, she made him write just as often! Over morning coffee, they sat at the kitchen table and each wrote two letters — one to Ted and one to me. My camp counselors called me a "mail hog" because I got eighteen letters in five days! It was wonderful. Teddy got just as many.

My favorite letter all week long was to "Jen-Jen" from Paul. On the stationery he drew a fluorescent blue heart around one "Jen" and a fluorescent green heart around the other. Paul's news was exciting. He had decided to move into an apartment behind our house in mid-autumn. Then, he said Ted and I could pop in on him after school or whenever we wanted. We would eat popcorn and watch movies — no homework allowed! On weekends there would be pajama parties until dawn. I especially liked Paul's promise to tell my parents we had gone to bed on time. Of course, Mom and

Dad would never believe him; but they wouldn't fuss, either. Paul is our buddy and they would want us to have fun with him as long as possible.

Mom said afterwards that Paul's week with them had been a gift. By the time Teddy and I returned from camp at the end of the week, my uncle was very sick. Paul was in terrific pain and was very white. Teddy was so scared when he first saw Paul that he hid behind Dad. It's not that Paul looked tremendously different; it's just that my brother was frightened. It was the first time it truly hit him that Paul was dying.

Dad, Ted, and I drove Paul home to New York City. That was the last time I ever saw him and the last time I was ever with him. If only I had known.... It is strange and sad now that I think about it.... So much has happened since that Sunday in August.

By the next day, Paul was back in the hospital. Ever since, his life has not been the same. Neither has ours. Paul has spent more of the last six months in the hospital than in his apartment. I know he will never be well again. We are being dragged steadily down into a fast whirlpool from which Paul cannot escape.

Sixth grade started and so did cheerleading. School is awesome; home is depressing.

Dear Diary,

Just sitting in my room, trying to do my homework. Can't concentrate on it right now. Just thinking about Paul. I really miss all the fun times with him. It has been awhile since Paul has been well enough to be outrageous with us. I don't want to believe that my favorite uncle in the whole wide world is dying. I don't want to believe he is suffering from AIDS. Yet I know he is usually in a lot of pain. I love Paul and he loves me. That's part of what makes his dying so hard. I can't imagine not having him around anymore.

Thanks for listening. Gotta do my homework now.

Jen-Jen

Yes, part of Paul's dying is losing him. The other part is that I am scared to death my friends will discover he has AIDS. They know my uncle is dying and that our life is very stressful right now. Fortunately, they haven't asked me directly what is wrong with him. I don't want to lie. Yet I am afraid to tell the truth. I know better — I hear what goes on at school.

24

The entire situation makes me mad and sad and scared. I desperately want my friends' support, but I am frightened. I am afraid my friends will reject me if they know Paul has AIDS. I am scared I will lose them and that I will be alone. I am afraid my friends' parents won't let their children play with me anymore. I am frightened by what they will think of me and how they will treat me. So I stay silent. It is absolutely terrible to live in silent fear. I know. I've been doing it for months.

The sad part is that I really don't understand why it has to be this way. I am only eleven years old. I haven't done anything wrong. I am a good person. Paul is also a wonderful person. Like everyone else, he deserves kindness and understanding. Paul does have a terrible disease, but people cannot catch AIDS from him if they are careful. Certainly no one can get AIDS from me just because my uncle has AIDS. Why do many people treat AIDS patients so viciously? Why should I have to fear that friends or strangers will treat me like an outcast?

Dear Diary,

School was horrible today. During recess I heard one of my classmates tease another kid. He was so cruel. He

> shouted, "You're fat. You're ugly. You
> have AIDS." Most of the kids laughed. I
> didn't. I walked away with tears in my
> eyes. Why did he say that?
>
> I'm even more scared after today. If
> everyone knew my "secret," how would
> they treat me? Tonight I can't stop crying.
>
> Jenny

When I tell my parents what kids in school say about AIDS, they are very sad for me. It makes them angry that, through no fault of my own, I could be ridiculed by my peers. Mom and Dad understand my fear that the news of Paul's AIDS could race around school like wildfire. They appreciate my fear that I could be the target of peer abuse. Because of me, my parents stay quiet about Paul. They would rather not, but they don't want to put me in danger.

Many adults aren't very sympathetic about AIDS. I guess it is hard for kids to be much better. Even one of my own relatives has not supported Paul. A letter was written in Dad's family requesting "anyone with AIDS" to stay away from holiday gatherings. Boy, did that hurt Paul! If my own family turns him away, what can he expect from others?

So, I keep my tears from my friends and my mouth shut in school. I don't say a word in class when we talk about AIDS, although I have a ton to share — and a ton I *want* to share. My stomach churns every time I hear rude remarks on the playground or in the halls about AIDS. So, I turn for comfort from Mom, Dad, and my faithful diary, instead of my friends. How I miss the help from my friends....

If only my friends knew what AIDS people are really like. AIDS patients are good people just like Paul. They are people from "nice" families — just like us. They are people with feelings and hopes and fears — just like us. They are people who want to be accepted and loved — just like us. They are people who are afraid of ridicule and rejection and scorn — just like us. They are people who want to belong and to be included — just like us. If only my friends knew how horrible it is to die from AIDS and to live in fear of dying as an outcast. If only they knew how much I hurt inside because of all that is happening. Perhaps then I could feel safe turning to them for help and support. Then I wouldn't have to keep my "shocking secret" to myself.

Dear Diary,
All right! Score one for Mom! This

> *morning the crew stopped by to pick me up for school. One of my friends walked into the kitchen and said, "Hey, did you hear the joke about the guy with AIDS?" I thought Mom would go through the roof! She snapped back, "There are no jokes. And I certainly will NOT listen to an AIDS joke. That is no joking matter." I could have kissed her. My friends really like my mother and call her "Mom" to her face. Boy, did my friend shut up in a hurry when Mom said that. It was wonderful. Yahoo!*
>
> *Love,*
> *Jen-Jen*

Sixth grade is in full swing. The first marking period is almost over. I am happy that the work is not too overwhelming. For the most part, I like my teachers. Almost all of my close friends are in my class so my days are lots of fun. Those who aren't with me, I see after school or I talk to on the phone. I don't have a boyfriend this year...so far...but some of the guys look interesting! And, yes, school is *definitely* better being "King of the Hill." On the other hand, home is *definitely* worse. If only home could be like it used to be. Then everything would be "King of the Hill."

My parents go to New York almost every week-end, and Dad travels there during the week for emergencies. It seems that more and more crises arise with each passing day. Our phone rings forever, at all hours, and it is not for me very often. Dad tells me he spends more time being a brother these days than a father. Boy, that's the truth. Paul does have wonderful friends in New York City who help him a great deal on a day-to-day basis. He is very lucky. So are we. Yet, he gets such comfort from my parents; and he lives from week-end-to-weekend to see them. There really is no one else who can help Paul the way Mom and Dad do. My great-grandmother is an enormous assistance, but she is eighty-six years old and cannot travel very well. So, the main tasks fall on my parents' shoulders. No wonder they are weary most of the time. It cannot be easy juggling a job, a family, and a dying brother in another state...let alone your feelings.

I try very hard to be understanding, but some-times I feel *angry*. I feel angry that Paul is sick. I feel very angry that my parents are away from me so much — and have been for months. I know in my head that Mom and Dad can't help it, but somehow that makes no difference. I want to shout, "Enough is enough!" I am sick and tired of being farmed out every weekend. My aunts, my tiny grandmother, and my godparents help quite a bit. I love them all dearly, but I want my parents. I just plain miss them.

I know Mom and Dad work hard to keep our lives as normal as possible. I know my parents worry about Teddy and me. I know they do the best they can and juggle everything the best they can. Yet, after a while, I just don't care. I *am* angry at my parents and I *am* angry at my uncle.

I know it is ridiculous to feel angry at Paul for being sick. So then I feel guilty. My life is an emotional roller coaster these days. I have a ton of different feelings racing up the track, down the track, and in a big loop-de-loop. I just wish this nightmare would go away.

Dear Diary,

Paul called tonight. He told my parents he is not moving into an apartment behind our house. Part of it is that he doesn't want to change doctors. A bigger part is that he isn't sure how our small town would treat him if it found out he has AIDS. I must admit that I don't know of anyone in town who has AIDS. I think Paul has reason to worry.

Paul told my parents he is afraid of

being rejected. He is also very scared that Ted and I will be rejected. Paul is not willing to take these chances. I wonder why my parents don't worry about that, especially Dad because he's a judge. People throughout the county know him well. How can my parents be brave enough to face everyone if the news becomes public knowledge? I know I'm not.

The longer this goes on, the more confused I become. And the more scared I become. I am afraid of questions I don't want to answer. There is no doubt that Paul is closer to death. It is weird, but I never knew it took so long to die. There is so much I don't understand.

Thanks for listening.

Love,
Jenny

Halloween was absolutely fantastic. We carved five pumpkins again this year even though Paul was not with us. He was happy knowing we had carved one for him. "Paul's" pumpkin looked *so* much better this year. But the best news is that I got my revenge. I won the pumpkin carving contest! Once more our house looked terrific all aglow with Jack-o-lanterns in the front windows.

My four girlfriends and I all decided to wear poodle skirts for Halloween. Mom called us the "Poodle Patrol." I loved the skirt Mom made for me — light blue with a fuzzy white poodle on a gold leash. It looked like the real thing from the 1950's! None of my big, baggy sweaters looked right with the poodle skirt, so I borrowed a top from my tiny grandmother. It was just the right size for the fashion of the '50s! The entire gang dressed at my house. We stuffed ourselves on pepperoni pizza before trick-or-treating. Oh, Halloween was great fun!

Thank goodness I didn't have to trick-or-treat with Teddy. It's not that I don't like him; it just wouldn't have been the same. Ted went as Robin Hood. We took a great picture of my brother in his forest green tights before he put on his tunic. Ooh-la-la! Mom dressed as a vampire to answer the door. Dad wore a glow-in-the-dark Jason mask to walk around with Ted and his friends. Halloween is usually fun at my house. I'm glad it was this year. We certainly needed a happy distraction from the problems with Paul.

As I look back on the fall of sixth grade, it seems it dragged on *forever.* There were endless trips to New York and endless hours on the phone. Mom and Dad tried really hard to be upbeat for Ted and me, but Paul's illness was very difficult for them personally. The sicker and weaker Paul became, the sadder they became. There was so much stress at home. Sometimes my parents cried without warning. They usually looked tired and weary and sad. I guess that's because they were. School was a great escape for me. Thank goodness I liked it.

Dear Diary,

Tonight Mom and I went to the mall just for the heck of it. I know she wanted to get out of the house, and I'm ALWAYS up for shopping! I love the mall!

It turned out to be a strange evening. We were at a check-out counter buying an oldies tape and, the next thing I knew, Mom was crying. She quickly gave me money to pay for the tape and ran out of the store. Boy, I had no idea what was happening. One minute we were having fun and the next minute she was crying. I bought the tape and found Mom sitting on a bench outside the store. There were tears streaming down her face. She smiled sadly at me and told me the song in the store reminded her of Paul — when they used to go dancing. I gave her a great big hug and she held on tightly.

As we walked around, I kept checking her for tears. It bothers me when she cries because I don't know how to help her. The only thing I know to do is to hug her. She tells me that my hugs are fantastic. It is awkward for me when my parents are so sad. I'm used to them being strong and, all of a sudden, they aren't. Sometimes I feel stronger than they are. Things are backwards these days.

Tonight I finally asked her what has been bothering me for a while. Because it is certain that Paul is going to die, wouldn't it have been better if he had died right away? Mom froze right in the middle of the mall and looked at me in amazement. She told me how wise and understanding I was. Mom said it would have been dreadful to lose Paul quickly. But in many ways it would have been a blessing, especially for Paul. It is so difficult for him to suffer through a long and painful death.

I hope it never happens to me.

You are a wonderful listener, Diary.

JJ

This Thanksgiving we did something totally different. My family went to New York to see the annual parade of giant balloons. We met my aunt, her family, and my tiny grandmother in the City. I really do love my mom's family, and my cousins are true friends. Getting to New York was an eerie adventure. In order to get curbside seats, we left home before the sun rose. It was ghostly leaving town when most people were asleep. By the time we got to New Jersey, we had seen only five cars on the road! As we drove down 42nd Street in The Big Apple, the sun was just bursting over the horizon. Soon the street was flooded with brilliance. It was quite a sight. Dad still talks about it.

After hooking up with my relatives, we found an empty curb for ten on Broadway. The long wait for the parade began. Was it ever cold and windy that day! Holy mackerel! My three cousins and I piled onto two beach chairs, huddled under blankets, and tried to stay warm. Teddy draped himself on top of us and went to sleep! We bought hot chocolate and sang Christmas carols to pass the time. Actually, the long wait was a ton of fun — and definitely worth it.

The balloons were unbelievably enormous! They towered high above the streets and sidewalks much more than I ever dreamed. Ted's favorite was Spider Man who posed in his famous crawling position. Babar was new this year. He floated along in the basket of a colorful hot air balloon dressed in his traditional green suit. I personally liked Betty Boop perched on her shimmering crescent moon! Poor Kermit the Frog ripped his right shoulder during the parade. He looked rather pathetic with his skinny green body drooping on one side.

It amazed me how hard the balloon handlers worked in the wind. At times they really struggled — actually bent over in half — to drag the balloons against the gusts. The balloons bounced around way up high in the street! Sometimes they blew into buildings. Other times they crashed into light fixtures or bent lamp posts on the tops of buildings. The whole crowd went wild and yelled, "Whooooaaaa!" every time a balloon veered out of control. The weather certainly made the day much more exciting! It was fantastic.

By the time Santa and his eight reindeer brought up the end of the parade, we were just about frozen. Ted and I gratefully went back to my aunt's hotel room to get warm and to grab a quick snooze. It had already been a very long day. Mom and Dad went downtown to visit Paul in the hospital for a few hours. They were the only company he had on Thanksgiving Day. It is hard to imagine being alone in the hospital on Thanksgiving. My parents said Paul did not even think of it as a special day. It was just another day of dreadful suffering and

worry. How can it be that Paul didn't think of it as Thanksgiving? I don't understand.

That night we all met again at a hotel and stuffed ourselves on an enormous Thanksgiving buffet. The food tables went on forever! Even Mom and Dad had fun. It seemed like the good old days. I was thankful for Thanksgiving. I was thankful for my relatives. I was thankful for my health. It was a wonderful day. What a relief!

Dear Diary,

It isn't fair. On top of everything else, Paul needs an emergency operation to remove his gall bladder. The doctors weren't sure he would survive the procedure. Dad rushed to New York to be with Paul. We waited by the phone...for hours. When Dad finally called, the news was good and bad. Paul had pulled through. But his gall bladder was loaded with a deadly virus, CMV. Actually, CMV is throughout his body. It is an "opportunistic" infection. Now Paul has two of them....

Paul is in a panic; my parents are trying to calm him down. I am in a panic. Everything is falling apart...fast.

Love, Jen-Jen

Thanksgiving always starts our mad dash to Christmas. Oh, how I love December! I really enjoy the special holiday traditions we have in our family. Mom hangs fresh mistletoe with a red satin ribbon in a special spot in the house. Each year we try very hard to catch Teddy under it. Oh, does he howl and squirm when we manage to catch him off guard! He hates being kissed and maintains that he is *never* getting married. Huh! I'm going to remind my brother of his foolish statement in a few years.

Once again, Mom tortured us with her usual thirty dozen Christmas cookies. She is a fantastic chef when she puts her mind to it. Christmas is one of the few times all year that she really bakes. It is such a treat! I think I gain a billion pounds every Christmas.

Mom also made her red apple wreath for the door just like they do in Williamsburg. One morning we discovered a huge hunk bitten out of one of the apples. It looked like a hungry horse had sneaked up to our door and attacked the wreath! Did we ever snicker! The wreath looked totally ridiculous. Mom was tempted to leave the wreath in its nibbled condition to amuse the mailman and the neighbors. Finally she fixed it with a new rosy apple. Months later Teddy admitted to being the wreath prankster! I should have known.

Dear Diary,

Today we went to the tree farm to chop down our Christmas tree. My tiny grandmother went with us. She always does. Boy, is it a HASSLE getting everyone to agree on the same tree! Teddy sure was in a lousy mood. He ended up pouting down by the creek because we didn't choose his tree. I wish I had an older brother instead of a younger one....

Ted is generally in a bad mood these days. He is certain that Santa isn't bringing him the only thing he wants — a Super Nintendo. Hate to say it, but I think he is right on that one. Teddy doesn't even want Christmas to come! He is that afraid of being disappointed. Not me, I can't wait!

Later today we decorated gingerbread men and gingerbread houses for the Christmas tree. I love doing that. Mom's designs are always the best. It took us hours to get all the ornaments on the tree. I love playing with the decorations, especially the miniature nutcrackers and the tiny coffee grinder with a teeny gray mouse inside it. That is my favorite one.

> *The tree looks as beautiful as ever —*
> *down to the candy canes and baby's*
> *breath that go on last.*
>
> *It was a great day. Only two weeks 'til*
> *Christmas.*
>
>

See ya!
Jenny

Dad told us he planned to visit Paul on Christmas Day. Yes, my uncle is back in the hospital — on the AIDS floor once again. He hardly gets home before he returns. I was not wild about the idea of Dad leaving on Christmas, but I understood. I was *so* relieved when Mom said she would stay home. I was afraid she would go with him.

I have never visited Paul in the hospital. Children my age aren't allowed on the hospital floors. Besides, Paul doesn't want Teddy and me to see him in his present condition. I always wondered how I would feel being on a floor, surrounded by all AIDS patients. I think it would feel very strange. Mom and Dad say it is very sad. Everyone is at different stages of dying, but everyone is dying. Well, if I couldn't visit Paul, I was happy Mom was staying with us. I didn't want to be farmed out on December 25. As it is, it will be weird with Dad gone part of Christmas Day.

> *Dear Diary,*
>
> *Christmas is my favorite time of year, but it is hard being happy when death is looming. This is so difficult. I never realized how sad I could feel. It certainly is not a merry Christmas.*
>
> *Jenny*

Even so, our Christmas Eve was fantastic. I was in a great mood all day. Christmas was around the corner! My godparents, their young children, and my tiny grandmother came for our huge, traditional feast. Mom always outdoes herself on Christmas Eve. But I sure wish she wouldn't make those ugly Brussels sprouts — YUCK! I hate them. I hate even seeing them! At least I don't have to eat them. Christmas Eve is Dad's favorite day of the year. He even wears his tuxedo for dinner! I wore my first pair of heels this year. I was thrilled when Mom and I bought them.

One of the best parts of December 24 is Elf Arko. Santa always sends Elf Arko around on Christmas Eve to check on us one last time. Elf Arko sneaks up to our house, leaves a few presents at the door, rings the doorbell, and scampers away. When we dash to the door, there is a bag and a note from him...but no Elf Arko. Every year we try to catch him, but we are never fast enough. Between all four kids, you would think we could manage to do so one year. We never do! Ted spends a lot of time Christmas Eve looking out windows and tiptoeing up to doors. He even prowls around outdoors in search of the sneaky elf. Sometimes we hear sleigh bells outside. I've even heard them — for real — and, truthfully, I'm never quite sure how that happens! Despite our hard efforts, we have yet to see Elf Arko. He is an extremely slippery fellow!

Every Christmas Eve, Santa calls to talk with the younger kids. I used to chat with him but not anymore. Teddy really likes to talk with Santa. He quizzes jolly old St. Nick about what is happening in our house. Somehow, Santa always knows. That never fails to astonish Teddy. This year Santa called from his sleigh phone! Isn't he getting modern with his new high tech equipment! Teddy asked him one last time for a Super Nintendo. Santa never directly answered him. Instead, he reminded Teddy to leave cookies, milk, and a carrot by the chimney. Teddy quickly hopped to Santa's request when he hung up the phone!

Dear Diary,
I could scream. It is 6 o'clock Christ-

*mas morning and I can't wake Mom and
Dad up for another hour! That's because
last year Ted and I woke them up at 1, 3,
and 5 o'clock in the morning. Boy, were
my parents unhappy that day! Hey, I
couldn't sleep!*

*But now I can't stand it! That clock
sure isn't moving. I've tried to read, but
that doesn't work. I just found a little gift
outside my door from Blitzen. It is cute —
a teeny, tiny ornament for the little artifi-
cial tree in my room. I see a small gift
outside Ted's door, but I'm not waking
him up this year. No way. He announced
last night that he didn't want to get up for
Christmas and that he was going right
back to bed after opening presents! He's
really worried about that Super Nintendo.
Oh, is that clock slow! I wonder if I could
turn it ahead? This is the longest hour of
my life!*

Jenny

What a day! Christmas was full of highs and
lows. Right on the button at 7:00, I burst into my
parents' room. They groaned but got up as prom-
ised. I let Mom wake up Teddy. Not only was he still

sleeping, but he did not even want to go downstairs. Ted was not a happy camper as he shuffled into the family room. Far from it. The dreaded day had arrived. Ted and I opened our stockings before heading to the presents under the tree.

The first gift Ted opened was his Super Nintendo! I swear I never saw his eyes pop out as far as they did when he opened that present from Santa. I was so shocked that I fell over on the floor. Teddy hugged and hugged his gift. Then he looked up to the ceiling and said sweetly, "Thank you, Santa, wherever you are!" Ted never went back to bed! "Santa" was good to me as well, and, as usual, Paul had sent money for our stockings.

Christmas morning was terrific. The rest was a bit confusing. Dad left for New York early in the afternoon, and Mom played games with us for a few hours. When she started cooking Christmas dinner, Ted and I roller bladed and played Super Nintendo. The day went by quickly and, actually, I didn't miss Dad as much as I thought I would. I was glad about that. By the time Dad returned home that night, Mom had placed two last gifts at the dinner table — one for Ted and one for me. Mom said they were not Christmas presents. I had no idea what they were, and I sure was curious.

Teddy and I picked up our gifts and joined our parents in the family room. When we opened the boxes, we each found a check for $250 from Paul!

I was speechless. I was stunned. I could not imagine having that much money. I did not know why Paul was giving us that much money, especially if it wasn't a Christmas present. I didn't know what to say. I looked at my parents for an explanation.

Dad told us that Paul had a very special plan for Teddy and me all autumn long. It was an idea he dreamed about constantly as he went in and out of the hospital. Paul was determined to take Teddy and me on a wild shopping spree in New York City to buy us whatever we wanted. It would just be the three of us — no parents — so none of our wishes would get vetoed. The thought of our shopping trip was one of the few things that made him happy and kept him going throughout the fall.

Paul had many wild ideas about where we might go and what we might buy. His thoughts changed constantly as he imagined things even bigger...and better...and shinier...and flashier. Dad told us that Paul's schemes distracted him as he lay in the hospital — day after day, week after week, month after month. They kept his mind off his pain and his problems. Paul's dreams got him through some particularly rough times.

However, Paul now realized he would never be well enough to take Teddy and me shopping. It just would not be possible because he was so weak and near death. Yet, my uncle wanted us to have our wild spree. Paul made my parents promise to take us shopping and to allow us to buy anything we wanted — just like it would have been with him. They agreed.

I was too stunned to say anything. I never expected anything like this. My insides churned with all kinds of mixed feelings. I was happy to have the money. I was happy that Paul loved me. I was miserable that Paul was dying. I was sad and angry to lose someone I loved so much.

Teddy was sad and angry too. He began crying very loudly and flung himself into Mom's lap. Ted threw Paul's check on the floor and shouted, "I don't want Paul's money. I want Paul." After he calmed down, Ted tearfully demanded to know why bad things were always happening to our family. I know he was referring to Paul, but he was also thinking about Pop Pop, my dad's father. Pop Pop died suddenly about two years ago. Now that Teddy mentioned it, it did seem that we had more than our share of problems. Mom explained that all families have difficult times — now just happened to be our turn.

I stopped to think about my friends. Mom was right. Many of them do have very tough problems. Some of my friends' parents are divorced. One of them lost her father to cancer when she was very little. Yes, my friends certainly do take their fair turn with sadness.

However, in one *huge* sense, Mom was *wrong*. At least my friends can talk about their problems. I can't. It is "all right" for my friends to talk about a divorce or a death from cancer. Sure, I talked about my Pop Pop dying, but I don't talk about my uncle dying from AIDS. I'm too afraid. I have heard what kids say about AIDS. I have heard how they mock and ridicule. I have heard how cruel they can be. I have good reason to fear what would happen if my peers knew my "secret." Yes, all families have problems, but most don't need to hide them from the world. It isn't fair and it isn't right that I feel I must. I don't like keeping all this agony inside me.

My family talked and cried a long time on Christmas night. Dinner burned.

Dear Diary,

Ha! It sure isn't taking Teddy long to spend his money from Paul! Actually, I am surprised it wasn't gone in a day. He ran out again today to buy another Super Nintendo game. I know it drives Mom crazy! But she keeps her end of the bargain and doesn't veto what he wants. I'm proud of her!

Ted called Paul tonight. He does whenever he buys something new. It always

47

*thrills Paul to hear of my brother's latest
purchase. I talked with Paul, too. Paul
asked me...again...if I have bought anything. I think he is disappointed because
I haven't. In all truthfulness, I'm always
at the mall, looking. But nothing excep-
tional catches my eye. I want to be
certain that what I buy is extra special.*

*Mya and I are going skiing this Friday
night. Only three days to go. That will be
great! I don't ski very often because Mom
is not home many weekends. I'm so
happy whenever I get on the slopes.*

Talk to you later.
Jenny

It's hard to imagine, but things absolutely wors-
ened in January. Paul can no longer do even the
simplest things for himself. He can't even get to the
bathroom without help. It has been weeks since he
has eaten anything normal. Paul receives "food"
through tubes and requires twenty-four hour nursing care. My beloved uncle is wasting away to
nothing. It is pretty obvious that little time re-
mains. He knows it, we know it, and his doctors
know it. Paul's biggest fear is to die in a hospital.
He asked whether he could come to our house to

die. Mom agreed right away; Dad asked to think about it; Ted ignored it; and I panicked.

Dear Diary,

Oh my gosh. What am I going to do? I love Paul, but I don't want him to die in my house. Mom and Dad are planning to set up our living room for Paul and his nurses. They told Ted and me that right now Paul's needs were more important than the family's needs.

I know I won't have to see him, but I am afraid to have him with us. Why does his AIDS seem riskier now that he is so close to death? I know I am not at risk for getting AIDS as long as I protect myself. I know Paul is no more "dangerous" than he was years ago. So why does it all seem so much worse now?

What am I going to tell my friends? They won't be able to pick me up for school or visit or sleep over as they usually do. What will I say if they ask questions? How long does it take someone to die? What will it be like to have someone die in my house? How will I sleep with nurses in and out of the house

> *24 hours a day? What will it be like to hear someone in pain?*
>
> *I always thought this day would never come. I am really scared.*
>
> *Jenny*

I told my parents my fears. They understood all of them. My worries were the same ones that Dad wanted to consider before he agreed Paul could come. On the one hand, I am really proud of my parents for sticking by Paul. As I mentioned, not everyone in my family has accepted my uncle. I always thought that was lousy. Paul was forever relieved that Mom and Dad never turned their backs on him, even though he never expected them to. He knows many AIDS patients who have no family support. I can't imagine dying alone without anybody by your side — just because of the type of disease you have. That is really sad. I truly appreciate why Paul loves my parents so much. They have been super in many, many ways. On the other hand, I am only eleven; and I am not as brave as they are.

As it turned out, it didn't matter anyway. Paul was too weak and too sick to travel from New York to Pennsylvania. He decided to die in his apartment. He decided never to return to the hospital.

And...he decided NOW was the time to die. My heart flew into my throat when I heard that. How do you ever make a decision like that? How do you ever decide you can't go on living?

Dear Diary,

I know the end is very near. Yesterday Dad drove my great-grandmother to New York to see Paul. She seldom travels anymore, but Dad told her it was now or never to say good-bye. When Dad returned, he asked Teddy and me if we wanted to see Paul one last time. I said, "No." Ted said, "Yes."

Ted has many interesting questions about Paul. He must think about Paul quite a bit. Teddy especially wants to know what Paul looks like. Today he asked Mom whether Paul looked like a monster or whether he was green. We never saw my Pop Pop after he died. Teddy cannot figure out what a dead or dying person looks like.

I want to remember Paul the way he was — when he was full of life.

Jen-Jen

In January, Mom and I stayed home while Dad and Ted went to New York to say good-bye. I was all ears when they returned. Paul had not had a good day, so they did not visit long — just long enough to say good-bye. Mom asked Teddy how Paul looked — whether he looked like a monster. I still remember his answer. "Well," said Ted, "he looks like Paul, but he is very pale. I didn't cry, Mom, even though I wanted to. I tried really hard not to cry." Mom told Teddy it would have been just fine for him to cry. Ted replied, "I know, but I didn't want to upset Paul." I thought my brother was very brave to visit Paul. It took a lot of courage.

Dear Diary,

Yes! I am so excited. Mya invited me to go skiing with her family for a week in Vermont! I'll be getting out of here — and out of school! I don't know which is better! And just think — a whole week with no Ted and no parents and no problems and no classes. Yes! Yes! Yes! It will be heaven! I already picked up my homework for the week. Holy cow! Sixth grade sure piles it on big time! Guess it will be worth it.

> *Gotta pack! Gotta pray for snow!*
>
> *Jen*

What a week! The skiing was fantastic and our ski instructor was absolutely gorgeous. Mya and I even got up our courage to snowboard for the first time. Boy, is it hard! I fell a billion times and got a billion bruises! But it was worth it. We had such a blast. I forgot all my problems — until I walked into my home a week later.

My parents were gone and my tiny grandmother had moved in a few days before. While I was away, Mom and Dad had dropped everything and virtually were living in New York. They didn't tell me they were going to Paul's apartment when I had called home. They didn't want to ruin my trip. I was very disappointed when they weren't home. I was bursting with news about my trip. And...there we went...again. When is it going to end?

The word from New York was grim. The doctors did not expect Paul to live more than a few days. Still, I didn't know whether or not to believe that *this time* Paul was really going to die. We had heard the words *"this time"* so often before that we stopped jumping at them. That's part of what has made this all so difficult. My heart has been in my throat so often — yet Paul is still alive. Many times

53

in the fall we thought Paul would be dead in week, but he always managed to pull through each crisis. He fought so hard in the past that I wasn't quite certain that *this* was *the* time. However, my parents had never been gone for days before. And Paul had never decided *now* was the time to die. These were not good signs.

Even with the doctor's prediction, Paul lived longer than expected. This made it extra hard on both Paul and my parents who were together quite a bit his final two weeks in February. Mom and Dad spent hours sitting by his bed in his apartment, holding his hand as he lay dying. They shared stories and good-byes. They cried and they laughed. Mom and Dad came home every few days weary and exhausted, only to catch their breath and return to New York. I don't know how they did it.

Dear Diary,

Tonight I finally spent some of Paul's money. I had been searching for something very special for weeks, and, at last, it caught my eye. When I told Mom and Dad what I wanted to buy, they were speechless. Mom became teary-eyed. She dropped everything and drove me to the mall immediately.

A few days ago I had seen what I wanted to buy. It was the most beautiful, golden heart-shaped locket hanging on a long golden chain. On the front of the locket were two entwined hearts — one for Paul and one for me — surrounded by wisps of leaves and branches. I knew right away it was meant for me. I knew right away it was Paul's gift to me.

The locket was still in the jewelry case in the store, just waiting for me. I held it in my hands and smiled. Mom smiled, too. I had Paul's initials engraved on the back of the locket before I put it on. Soon I will put our pictures inside.

I called Paul tonight to tell him about "our" locket. He was very touched and very quiet. Paul finally whispered, "Oh, Jen-Jen." I know he never expected me to buy something like this. I am glad he lived long enough to know about my locket. Now he will always be with me.

I am wearing my locket to bed. I want to wear it every day.

Jen-Jen

Valentine's Day is always special in our house. I love waking up on February 14 because Mom and Dad make it so much fun. In the morning Teddy and I find a big shiny Valentine balloon tied to our chairs at the kitchen table and a little gift at our seat. This year, Valentine's Day was going to be extra terrific. It was on a Friday and we had off from school for teacher in-service. On top of that, I was going skiing with two friends and it had snowed three inches overnight!

I jumped out of bed, double-checked the snow out my window and ran downstairs. I found my balloon and a little gift — a new paperback book — waiting for me in the kitchen. The day was off to a terrific start. The skiing was going to be fantastic. It was!

Mom picked up the gang at the ski slope late in the afternoon on Valentine's Day. Was she ever on edge. The nurse had told her that Paul would not live through the weekend. My parents were heading into New York the next day and Mom wanted to be with Paul when something happened. Just as importantly, she did not want him to die on Valentine's Day. Mom kept "telling" Paul to hang on for a few more hours. Every time the phone rang, Mom jumped. It seemed to ring all night long. The mood of the house was tense and uneasy.

At 8:10 on Valentine's night the phone rang once again. It was the nurse. Yes, Paul had just

died five minutes before. When my parents walked into the family room, they did not have to tell Teddy and me the news. We could tell by their faces that Paul was dead. They nodded their heads "yes," but I did not want to believe them. It was Valentine's Day. I was not wearing my locket because I had been skiing.

Ted threw himself onto the sofa and cried out his heart. Mom rubbed his back for him. As he cried, Ted sobbed, "At least Paul is with Pop Pop now." I sat by myself — very still and very straight like a statue. I felt one lone tear run down my cheek, but that was all. I could not believe Paul was dead.

I miss Paul terribly. I wish I could talk to my friends about him, but I am afraid to tell them the truth. I am afraid of their response. I am afraid they will reject me. I am afraid they will tease me. I am afraid they will no longer be my friends.

I wish I could tell my friends how sad this has been for me. I wish I could tell them how upsetting it was to see my parents so incredibly sad and not know how to help them. I wish I could tell them what it was like to lose my parents for months while they constantly cared for my uncle in another state. I wish I could tell them what it was like every time the phone rang, not knowing who or what it was. I wish I could tell them how scary AIDS is and how afraid I was...and still am...not quite understanding everything that happened. I wish I could tell them the truth.

I can't. My uncle had AIDS.

> *Dear Diary,*
>
> *I guess it was meant to be that Paul died on Valentine's Day. He and my locket will be special forever.*
>
> *I love you, Paul. Maybe now it is time to tell our story.*
>
> *Love,*
Jen-Jen

Christine Simpson is a nationally certified school psychologist who has worked directly with thousands of children in schools. She is an active HIV prevention/sensitivity presenter, speaking to assemblies, professional groups, conventions, and community forums, and appearing on radio and television. In addition, as a consultant with a national firm, she trains and presents throughout the country concerning numerous educational, clinical, and interpersonal issues. Christine has authored professional texts and materials, as well as other children's books. She lives with her husband and two children in Nazareth, Pennsylvania.